Dear Parents and Educators,

Welcome to Penguin Young Readers! As parents and educators, you know that each child develops at his or her own pace—in terms of speech, critical thinking, and, of course, reading. Penguin Young Readers recognizes this fact. As a result, each Penguin Young Readers book is assigned a traditional easy-to-read level (1–4) as well as a Guided Reading Level (A–P). Both of these systems will help you choose the right book for your child. Please refer to the back of each book for specific leveling information. Penguin Young Readers features esteemed authors and illustrators, stories about favorite characters, fascinating nonfiction, and more!

Owls: Birds of the Night

LEVEL **3**

GUIDED READING LEVEL **L**

This book is perfect for a **Transitional Reader** who:
- can read multisyllable and compound words;
- can read words with prefixes and suffixes;
- is able to identify story elements (beginning, middle, end, plot, setting, characters, problem, solution); and
- can understand different points of view.

Here are some **activities** you can do during and after reading this book:
- Comprehension: After reading the book, answer the following questions:
  - What do owls eat?
  - What is an owl pellet? Why do scientists study them?
  - How many types of owls are there? Name several and where they live.
  - Explain how owls learn to fly.
  - How can you help protect owls?
- Make Connections: Have you ever seen an owl? If so, where did you see it and what did the owl look like? Write a paragraph about a time when you saw or heard an owl. If you have never seen an owl, use some facts you learned in this book to write a paragraph about what it would be like to see an owl.

Remember, sharing the love of reading with a child is the best gift you can give!

—Bonnie Bader, EdM
  Penguin Young Readers program

*Penguin Young Readers are leveled by independent reviewers applying the standards developed by Irene Fountas and Gay Su Pinnell in *Matching Books to Readers: Using Leveled Books in Guided Reading*, Heinemann, 1999.

To my own fledglings, Lucy and William—ES

To my dear teachers, Liana Mertzani
and Yiannis Georgariou, who helped me
take my first steps as an artist—CR

PENGUIN YOUNG READERS
Published by the Penguin Group
Penguin Group (USA) LLC, 375 Hudson Street, New York, New York 10014, USA

USA | Canada | UK | Ireland | Australia | New Zealand | India | South Africa | China

penguin.com
A Penguin Random House Company

Photo credits: cover: © Wendi Evans/iStock/Getty Images; page 8: (forest): © David De Lossy/Digital Vision/Getty Images, (flying robin) © ivkuzmin/iStock/Getty Images, (flying bluebird) © Steve Byland/iStock/Getty Images, (bluejay left) © Els van der Gun/iStock/Getty Images, (bluejay right) © Jeff Cashdollar/iStock/Getty Images, (robin ground) © andreea staicu/iStock/Getty Images; page 9: (bat) © Purestock/Thinkstock/Getty Images, (owl) © AbleStock.com/Thinkstock/Getty Images, (coyote) © jtstewartphoto/iStock/Getty Images, (raccoon) © Tony Campbell/iStock/Getty Images; page 10: (skunk) © Eric Isselée/iStock/Getty Images, (rabbit) © Joshua Lewis/iStock/Getty Images, (mouse) © Sascha Burkard/iStock/Getty Images; (rat) © Dmitry Maslov/iStock/Getty Images, (squirrel) © Emily Churchill/iStock/Getty Images; page 15: © Dave King/Getty Images; page 16–17: (pygmy owl) © Patrick Kuyper/iStock/Getty Images, (spectacled owl) © garytog/iStock/Getty Images, (barn owl) © PhilEllard/iStock/Getty Images, (short-eared owl) © Peter Candido/iStock/Getty Images, (bay owl) © voraorn/iStock/Getty Images, (barking owl) © Angela Maloney/iStock/Getty Images, (pearl-spotted owl) © demerzel21/iStock/Getty Images, (map) © Michael Travers/Hemera/Getty Images; page 18–19: © (owl) © MikeLane45/iStock/Getty Images, (trees) © 29mokara/iStock/Getty Images; page 20: (elf owl) © Bowers Photo, (pear) © Anthony DOUANNE/iStock/Getty Images; page 26: © Purestock/Thinkstock/Getty Images; page 27: (top) © Daniel J. Cox/NaturalExposures.com, (bottom) © Adam Jones/Visuals Unlimited; page 28: © Vasiliy Vishnevski/Hemera/Getty Images; page 29: © Daniel J. Cox/NaturalExposures.com; page 30: © Daniel J. Cox/NaturalExposures.com; page 31: © Michael Quinton/Visuals Unlimited; page 35: © Design Pics/Thinkstock/Getty Images; page 44: (owl) © Joe McDonald/Visuals Unlimited, (tree) © Elena Elisseeva/iStock/Getty Images; page 45: © Brent Davis/iStock/Getty Images; page 46: © Bowers Photo; page 47: © Jupiterimages/Photos.com/Getty Images; page 48: © Mike Watson Images/moodboard/Getty Images.

Library of Congress Cataloging-in-Publication Data is available.

ISBN 978-0-448-48135-7 (pbk)   10 9 8 7 6 5 4 3 2 1
ISBN 978-0-448-48136-4 (hc)   10 9 8 7 6 5 4 3 2 1

PENGUIN YOUNG READERS

LEVEL
TRANSITIONAL READER
3

Owls
Birds of the Night

by Emily Sollinger
illustrated by Chris Rallis and with photographs

Penguin Young Readers
An Imprint of Penguin Group (USA) LLC

It is night.

The forest is dark and quiet.

Suddenly, a large bird silently
swoops down from a tree.
The bird is a great horned owl.
It is hunting for food.

Most birds, like robins and blue jays,
look for food during the day.

But owls are different.
They are nocturnal
(say: nok-TUR-nal).
They sleep during the day
and stay awake at night.
Some other nocturnal animals
are bats, raccoons, and coyotes.

Most birds eat seeds and nuts.

But not owls.

They eat other animals,

even other birds.

Owls eat rats, mice, rabbits,

squirrels, skunks, reptiles, frogs,

and spiders.

Owls have no trouble seeing
in the dark.

They can see things that are
very far away.

They also have sharp ears.

They can hear sounds from
very far away.

Their eyes and ears help owls
find food.

Look!

A field mouse is scurrying

along the ground.

The owl has spotted it.

Down swoops the owl.

In a flash it catches the mouse
in its talons.

It has four talons on each foot.

The owl opens its beak and swallows
the mouse whole.

The owl cannot digest
all of the mouse.
Many hours later,
it coughs up a dry wad
of teeth, fur, and bones.

This is called a pellet.

Scientists study owl pellets.

From them, they learn about what

owls eat and where they live.

There are more than 200 different kinds of owls.
They live all over the world.
The only place owls do not live is Antarctica.

BARN OWL

RIDGWAY'S PYGMY OWL

SPECTACLED OWL

SHORT-EARED OWL

ORIENTAL BAY OWL

BARKING OWL

PEARL-SPOTTED OWL

The biggest owl in North America
is the great gray owl.
From wing to wing,
it measures up to five feet.
But it only weighs three pounds.
That's because owls have
light, hollow bones.
All birds do.
Light bones help them lift off
the ground and fly.

The smallest owl is the elf owl.

It lives in the desert.

It is no bigger than a pear.

The strongest owl is
the great horned owl.
It can carry off animals
that are bigger than it is.
Its nickname is the "flying tiger."
That's because it's so strong
and fierce.

Owls have thick, strong feathers
so they can fly.
Once a year, the feathers
will start to fall out.
New ones will grow in.
This is called molting.
This is how the owl gets rid
of damaged feathers.
Molting takes about three months.

Have you ever heard an owl hoot?

Usually hoots are very loud.

A hoot may mean an owl is telling

other owls to stay away

from its home.

Or a hoot may mean that an owl

is looking for a mate.

Male and female owls call
to each other.
A male barred owl brings food
for the female.
This shows his interest in her.
Once owls choose their mates,
they usually stay together for life.

Soon the female barred owl is ready
to lay her eggs.
Owls do not build their own nests.
The female barred owl lays her eggs
in an empty hawk's nest.
She may add moss, twigs, or feathers
to make it cozy.

Eastern screech owls lay their eggs
in a hole in a tree.

Snowy owls lay their eggs
on the ground.

Burrowing owls lay their eggs
underground.

A group of owl eggs is called
a clutch.
Most female owls lay between
seven and nine eggs.

The female sits on her eggs
to keep them warm.
She will not go off hunting.
The male owl will find food for her.

In about 30 days,

the eggs begin to hatch.

Baby owls are called owlets.

There is a sharp point on the top

of their beaks.

This is called an egg tooth.

It breaks through the egg,
and out pops the owlet.

EGG TOOTH

At first owlets are very weak.

A layer of fluffy feathers,

called down,

keeps them warm.

The mother and father owls both
feed the babies.
They put food right
into the babies' beaks.

After a few weeks,

owlets are stronger.

They begin to grow

stronger feathers.

They must learn to take good care

of their feathers

so that they can fly well.

Owls clean and brush their feathers

with their talons and beaks.

This is called preening.

About a month later,

the owlets are ready

to leave the nest.

At first, owlets hop
from branch to branch.
They grab onto tree bark.
They wander around
on the ground.
They practice flapping their wings.

Look!

They are flying!

The owlets are now called fledglings
(say: FLEJ-lings).

The fledglings learn to hunt
for food.

Still they stay close to their parents.

Their parents protect them from
other animals.

This eastern screech owl hears
something.
It is a raccoon.
It is too close
to the fledglings.

The eastern screech owl dives
toward the raccoon
and scares it away.
Her fledglings are safe.

43

In another month or two,
the fledglings are full-grown.
Soon they will search for mates
of their own.
They will face many dangers.

In some areas,

owls' homes are being destroyed.

Forests are cut down to make way

for new neighborhoods.

People can help protect the places where owls live.

People build special owl boxes.

Owls can nest safely inside them.

If more people help owls stay safe,

there will be more owls for us

to watch and learn about.

The next time you are in the woods,

wait until night.

Then listen closely.

You just might hear an owl hooting!